HOMILIES ON THE PSALMS

Hilary of Poitiers

The primary condition of knowledge for reading the Psalms is the ability to see as whose mouthpiece we are to regard the Psalmist as speaking, and who it is that he addresses. For they are not all of the same uniform character, but of different authorship and different types. For we constantly find that the Person of God the Father is being set before us, as in that passage of the eighty-eighth Psalm: *I have exalted one chosen out of My people, I have found David My servant, with My holy oil have I anointed him. He shall call Me, You are my Father and the upholder of my salvation. And I will make him My first-born, higher than the kings of the earth* ; while in what we might call the majority of Psalms the Person of the Son is introduced, as in the seventeenth: *A people whom I have not known has served Me* ; and in the twenty-first: *they parted My garments among them and cast lots upon My vesture.* But the contents of the first Psalm forbid us to understand it either of the Person of the Father or of the Son: *But his will has been in the law of the Lord, and in His Law will he meditate day and night.* Now in the Psalm in which we said the Person of the Father is intended, the terms used are exactly appropriate, for instance: *He shall call Me, You are my Father, my God and the upholder of my salvation;* and in that one in which we hear the Son speaking, He proclaims Himself to be the author of the words by the very expressions He employs, saying, *A people whom I have not known has served Me.* That is to say, when the Father on the one hand says: *He shall call Me;* and the Son on the other

1

hand says: *a people has served Me,* they show that it is They Themselves Who are speaking concerning Themselves. Here, however, where we have *But his will has been in the Law of the Lord;* obviously it is not the Person of the Lord speaking concerning Himself, but the person of another, extolling the happiness of that man whose will is in the Law of the Lord. Here, then, we are to recognise the person of the Prophet by whose lips the Holy Spirit speaks, raising us by the instrumentality of his lips to the knowledge of a spiritual mystery.

2. And as he says this we must enquire concerning what man we are to understand him to be speaking. He says: *Happy is the man who has not walked in the counsel of the ungodly nor stood in the way of sinners, and has not sat in the seat of pestilence. But his will has been in the Law of the Lord, and in His Law will he meditate day and night. And he shall be like a tree planted by the rills of water, that will yield its fruit in its own season. His leaf also shall not wither, and all things, whatsoever he shall do, shall prosper.* I have discovered, either from personal conversation or from their letters and writings, that the opinion of many men about this Psalm is, that we ought to understand it to be a description of our Lord Jesus Christ, and that it is His happiness which is extolled in the verses following. But this interpretation is wrong both in method and reasoning, though doubtless it is inspired by a pious tendency of thought, since the whole of the Psalter is to be

referred to Him: the time and place in His life to which this passage refers must be ascertained by the sound method of knowledge guided by reason.

3. Now the words which stand at the beginning of the Psalm are quite unsuited to the Person and Dignity of the Son, while the whole contents are in themselves a condemnation of the careless haste that would use them to extol Him. For when it is said, *and his will has been in the Law of the Lord*, how (seeing that the Law was given by the Son of God) can a happiness which depends on his will being in the Law of the Lord be attributed to Him Who is Himself Lord of the Law? That the Law is His He Himself declares in the seventy-seventh Psalm, where He says: *Hear My Law, O My people: incline your ears unto the words of My mouth. I will open My mouth in a parable.* And the Evangelist Matthew further asserts that these words were spoken by the Son, when he says *For this cause spoke He in parables that the saying might be fulfilled: I will open My mouth in parables.* Matthew 13:35 The Lord then gave fulfilment in act to His own prophecy, speaking in the parables in which He had promised that He would speak. But how can the sentence, *and he shall be like a tree planted by the rills of water,*— wherein growth in happiness is set forth in a figure— be possibly applied to His Person, and a tree be said to be more happy than the Son of God, and the cause of His happiness, which would be the case if an analogy were established between Him and it in respect of

3

growth towards happiness? Again, since according to Wisdom Proverbs 8:22 and the Apostle, He is both before the ages and before times eternal, and is the First-born of every creature; and since in Him and through Him all things were created, how can He be happy by becoming like objects created by Himself? For neither does the power of the Creator need for its exaltation comparison with any creature, nor does the immemorial age of the First-born allow of a comparison involving unsuitable conditions of time, as would be the case if He were compared to a tree. For that which shall be at some point of future time cannot be looked upon as having either previously existed or as now existing anywhere. But whatsoever already is does not need any extension of time to begin existence, because it already possesses continuous existence from the date of its beginning up till the present.

4. And so, since these words are understood to be inapplicable to the divinity of the Only-begotten Son of God, our Lord Jesus Christ, we must suppose him, who is here extolled as happy by the Prophet, to be the man who strives to conform himself to that body which the Lord assumed and in which He was born as man, by zeal for justice and perfect fulfilment of all righteousness. That this is the necessary interpretation will be shown as the exposition of the Psalm proceeds.

5. The Holy Spirit made choice of this magnificent and noble introduction to the Psalter, in order to stir up weak man to a pure zeal for piety by the hope of happiness, to teach him the mystery of the Incarnate God, to promise him participation in heavenly glory, to declare the penalty of the Judgment, to proclaim the two-fold resurrection, to show forth the counsel of God as seen in His award. It is indeed after a faultless and mature design that He has laid the foundation of this great prophecy ; His will being that the hope connected with the happy man might allure weak humanity to zeal for the Faith; that the analogy of the happiness of the tree might be the pledge of a happy hope, that the declaration of His wrath against the ungodly might set the bounds of fear to the excesses of ungodliness, that difference in rank in the assemblies of the saints might mark difference in merit, that the standard appointed for judging the ways of the righteous might show forth the majesty of God.

But let us now deal with the subject matter and the words which express it.

6. *Happy is the man who has not walked in the counsel of the ungodly nor stood in the way of sinners, and has not sat in the seat of pestilence. But his will has been in the Law of the Lord, and in His Law will he meditate day and night.*

The Prophet recites five kinds of caution as continually present in the mind of the happy man: the first, not to walk in the counsel of the ungodly, the second, not to stand in the way of sinners, the third, not to sit in the seat of pestilence, next, to set his will in the Law of the Lord, and lastly, to meditate therein by day and by night. There must, therefore, be a distinction between the ungodly and the sinner, between the sinner and the pestilent; chiefly because here the ungodly has a counsel, the sinner a way, the pestilent a seat, and again, because the question is of walking, not standing, in the counsel of the ungodly; of standing, not walking, in the way of the sinner. Now if we would understand the reason of these facts, we must note the precise difference between the sinner and the undutiful , that so it may become clear why to the sinner is assigned a way, and to the undutiful a counsel; next, why the question is of standing in the way, and of walking in the counsel, whereas men are accustomed to connect standing with a counsel, and walking with a way.

Not every man that is a sinner is also undutiful: but the undutiful man cannot fail to be a sinner. Let us take an instance from general experience. Sons, though they be drunken and profligate and spendthrift, can yet love their fathers; and with all these vices, and, therefore, not free from guilt, may yet be free from undutifulness. But the undutiful, though they may be models of continence and frugality, are, by the mere fact of despising the parent, worse transgressors than if they were guilty of every sin that lies outside the category of undutifulness.

7. There is no doubt then that, as this instance proves, the undutiful (or ungodly) must be distinguished from the sinner. And, indeed, general opinion agrees to call those men ungodly who scorn to search for the knowledge of God, who in their irreverent mind take for granted that there is no Creator of the world, who assert that it arrived at the order and beauty which we see by chance movements, who, in order to deprive their Creator of all power to pass judgment on a life lived rightly or in sin, will have it that man comes into being and passes out of it again by the simple operation of a law of nature.

Thus, all the counsel of these men is wavering, unsteady, and vague, and wanders about in the same familiar paths and over the same familiar ground, never finding a resting-place, for it fails to reach any definite decision. They have never in their system risen to the doctrine of a Creator of the world, for instead of answering our questions as to the cause, beginning, and duration of the world, whether the world is for man, or man for the world, the reason of death, its extent and nature, they press in ceaseless motion round the circle of this godless argument and find no rest in these imaginings.

8. There are, besides, other counsels of the ungodly, i.e., of those who have fallen into heresy, unrestrained by the laws of either the New Testament or the Old. Their reasoning ever takes the course of a vicious circle; without grasp or foothold to stay them they tread their interminable round of endless indecision. Their ungodliness consists in measuring God, not by His own revelation, but by a standard of their choosing; they forget that it is as godless to make a God as to deny Him; if you ask them what effect these opinions have on their faith and hope, they are perplexed and confused, they wander from the point and wilfully avoid the real issue of the debate. Happy is the man then who has not walked in this kind of counsel of the ungodly, nay, who has not even entertained the wish to walk therein, for it is a sin even to think for a moment of things that are ungodly.

9. The next condition is, that the man who has not walked in the counsel of the ungodly shall not stand in the way of sinners. For there are many whose confession concerning God, while it acquits them of ungodliness, yet does not set them free from sin; those, for example, who abide in the Church but do not observe her laws; such are the greedy, the drunken, the brawlers, the wanton, the proud, hypocrites, liars, plunderers. No doubt we are urged towards these sins by the promptings of our natural instincts; but it is good for us to withdraw from the path into which we are being hurried and not to

stand therein, seeing that we are offered so easy a way of escape. It is for this reason that the man who has not stood in the way of sinners is happy, for while nature carries him into that way, religious belief draws him back.

10. Now the third condition for gaining happiness is not to sit in the seat of pestilence. The Pharisees sat as teachers in Moses' seat, and Pilate sat in the seat of judgment: of what seat then are we to consider the occupation pestilential? Not surely of that of Moses, for it is the occupants of the seat and not the occupation of it that the Lord condemns when He says: *The Scribes and Pharisees sit on Moses' seat; whatsoever they bid you do, that do; but do not ye after their work.* Matthew 23:2 The occupation of that seat is not pestilential, to which obedience is enjoined by the Lord's own word. That then must be really pestilential, the infection of which Pilate sought to avoid by washing his hands. For many, even God-fearing men, are led astray by the canvassing for worldly honours; and desire to administer the law of the courts, though they are bound by those of the Church.

But although they bring to the discharge of their duties a religious intention, as is shown by their merciful and upright demeanour, still they cannot escape a certain contagious infection arising from the business in which their life is spent. For the conduct of civil cases does not suffer them to be true to the holy principles of the Church's law, even though they wish it. And without abandoning their pious purpose they are compelled, against their will, by the necessary conditions of the seat they have won, to use, at one time invective, at another, insult, at another, punishment; and their very position makes them authors as well as victims of the necessity which constrains them, their system being as it were impregnated with the infection. Hence this title, *the seat of pestilence*, by which the Prophet describes their seat, because by its infection it poisons the very will of the religiously minded.

11. But the fact that he has not walked in the counsel of the ungodly, nor stood in the way of sinners, nor sat in the seat of pestilence, does not constitute the perfection of the man's happiness. For the belief that one God is the Creator of the world, the avoidance of sin by the pursuit of unassuming goodness, the preference of the tranquil leisure of private life to the grandeur of public position— all this may be found even in a pagan. But here the Prophet, in portraying in the likeness of God the man that is perfect— one who may serve as a noble example of eternal happiness— points to the exercise by him of no commonplace virtues, and to the words, *But his will has been in the Law of the Lord*, for the attainment of perfect happiness. To refrain from what has gone before is useless unless his mind be set on what follows, *But his will has been in the Law of the Lord*. The Prophet does not look for fear.

The majority of men are kept within the bounds of Law by fear; the few are brought under the Law by will: for it is the mark of fear not to dare to omit what it is afraid of, but of perfect piety to be ready to obey commands. This is why that man is happy whose will, not whose fear, is in the Law of God.

12. But then sometimes the will needs supplementing; and the mere desire for perfect happiness does not win it, unless performance wait upon intention. The Psalm, you remember, goes on: *And in His Law will he meditate day and night.* The man achieves the perfection of happiness by unbroken and unwearied meditation in the Law. Now it may be objected that this is impossible owing to the conditions of human infirmity, which require time for repose, for sleep, for food: so that our bodily circumstances preclude us from the hope of attaining happiness, inasmuch as we are distracted by the interruption of our bodily needs from our meditation by day and night. Parallel to this passage are the words of the Apostle, *Pray without ceasing.* 1 Thessalonians 5:17 As though we were bound to set at naught our bodily requirements and to continue praying without any interruption! Meditation in the Law, therefore, does not lie in reading its words, but in pious performance of its injunctions; not in a mere perusal of the books and writings, but in a practical meditation and exercise in their respective contents, and in a fulfilment of the Law by the works we do by night and day, as the

Apostle says: *Whether you eat or drink, or whatsoever ye do, do all to the glory of God.* 1 Corinthians 10:31 The way to secure uninterrupted prayer is for every devout man to make his life one long prayer by works acceptable to God and always done to His glory: thus a life lived according to the Law by night and day will in itself become a nightly and daily meditation in the Law.

13. But now that the man has found perfect happiness by keeping aloof from the counsel of the ungodly and the way of sinners and the seat of pestilence, and by gladly meditating in the Law of God by day and by night, we are next to be shown the rich fruit that this happiness he has won will yield him. Now the anticipation of happiness contains the germ of future happiness. For the next verse runs: *And he shall be like a tree planted beside the rills of water, which shall yield its fruit in its own season, whose leaf also shall not fall off.* This may perhaps be deemed an absurd and inappropriate comparison, in which are extolled a planted tree, rills of water, the yielding of fruit, its own time, and the leaf that falls not. All this may appear trivial enough to the judgment of the world. But let us examine the teaching of the Prophet and see the beauty that lies in the objects and words used to illustrate happiness.

14. In the book of Genesis Genesis 2:9, where the lawgiver depicts the paradise planted by God, we are shown that every tree is fair to look upon and good

for food; it is also stated that there stands in the midst of the garden a tree of Life and a tree of the knowledge of good and evil; next that the garden is watered by a stream that afterwards divides into four heads. The Prophet Solomon teaches us what this tree of Life is in his exhortation concerning Wisdom: *She is a tree of life to all them that lay hold upon her, and lean upon her.* Proverbs 3:18 This tree then is living; and not only living, but, furthermore, guided by reason; guided by reason, that is, in so far as to yield fruit, and that not casually nor unseasonably, but in its own season. And this tree is planted beside the rills of water in the domain of the Kingdom of God, that is, of course, in Paradise, and in the place where the stream as it issues forth is divided into four heads. For he does not say, *Behind the rills of water,* but, *Beside the rills of water,* at the place where first the heads receive each their flow of waters. This tree is planted in that place whither the Lord, Who is Wisdom, leads the thief who confessed Him to be the Lord, saying: *Verily I say unto you, today shall you be with Me in Paradise.* Luke 23:43 And now that we have shown upon prophetic warrant that Wisdom, which is Christ, is called the tree of Life in accordance with the mystery of the coming Incarnation and Passion, we must go on to find support for the strict truth of this interpretation from the Gospels. The Lord with His own lips compared Himself to a tree when the Jews said that He cast out devils in Beelzebub: *Either make the tree good,* said He, *and its fruit good; or else make the tree*

13

corrupt, and its fruit corrupt; for the tree is known by its fruit Matthew 12:33; because although to cast out devils is an excellent fruit, they said He was Beelzebab, whose fruits are abominable. Nor yet did He hesitate to teach that the power that makes the tree happy resided in His Person, when on the way to the Cross He said: *For if they do these things in the green tree, what shall be done in the dry* Luke 23:31 ? Declaring by this image of the green tree that there was nothing in Him that was subject to the dryness of death.

15. That happy man, then, will become like this tree when he shall be transplanted, as the thief was, into the garden and set to grow beside the rills of water: and his planting will be that happy new planting which cannot be uprooted, to which the Lord refers in the Gospels when He curses the other kind of planting and says: *Every planting that My Father has not planted shall be rooted up.* Matthew 15:13 This tree, therefore, will yield its fruits. Now in all other passages where God's Word teaches some lesson from the fruits of trees, it mentions them as making fruit rather than as yielding fruit, as when it says: *A good tree cannot make evil fruits* , and when in Isaiah the complaint about the vine is: *I looked that it should make grapes, and it made thorns.* Isaiah 5:2 But this tree will yield its fruits, being supplied with free-will and understanding for the purpose. For it will yield its fruits in its own season. And, pray, in what season? In the season, of course, of which the Apostle

speaks: *That He might make known unto you also the mystery of His Will, according to His good pleasure which He has purposed in Himself, in the dispensation of the fullness of time.* Ephesians 1:9 This, then, is the dispensation of time, by which is regulated the right moment of receiving, in the case of the recipients, and of giving, in that of the giver; for the giver has choice of the season. But delay in point of time depends upon the fullness of times. For the dispensation of yielding fruit waits upon the fullness of time. Now what, you ask, is this fruit that is to be dispensed? That assuredly of which this same Apostle is speaking when he says: *And He will change our vile body, that it may be fashioned like His glorious body.* Philippians 3:21 Thus He will give us those fruits of His which He has already brought to perfection in that man whom He has chosen to Himself who is portrayed under the image of a tree, whose mortality He has utterly done away and has raised him to share in His own immortality.

This man then will be happy like that tree, when at length he stands surrounded by the glory of God, being made like the Lord.

16. *But the leaf of this tree shall not fall off.* There is no ground for wonder that its leaves do not fall off, seeing that its fruits will not drop to the ground, either because they are forced off by ripeness, or shaken off by external violence, but it will yield them, distributing them by an act of reasoned

service. Now the spiritual significance of the leaves is made clear by a comparison based upon material objects. We see that leaves are made to sprout round the fruits about which they cluster, for the express purpose of protecting them, and of forming a kind of fence to the young and tender shoots. What the leaves signify, then, is the teaching of God's words in which the promised fruits are clothed. For it is these words that kindly shade our hopes, that shield and protect them from the rough winds of this world. These leaves, then, that is the words of God, shall not fall: for the Lord Himself has said: *Heaven and earth shall pass away, but My words shall not pass away* Matthew 24:35, for of the words that have been spoken by God not one shall fail or fall.

17. Now that the leaves of the tree we speak of are not valueless but are a source of health to the nations is testified by St. John in the Apocalypse, where he says: *And He showed me a river of water of life, bright as crystal, proceeding out of the throne of God and of the Lamb; in the midst of the street of it and on either side of the river the tree of life, bearing twelve manner of fruits, yielding its fruit every month: and the leaves of the tree are for the healing the nations* Revelation 22:1 .

Bodily manifestations so reveal the mysteries of heaven that, although matter by itself cannot convey the full spiritual meaning, yet to regard them only in their material aspect is to mutilate them. We should have expected to hear that there were trees, not one tree, standing on either side of the river shown to the saint. But because the tree of Life in the sacrament of Baptism is in every case one, supplying to those that come to it on every side the fruits of the apostolic message, so there stands on either side of the river one tree of Life. There is one Lamb seen amid the throne of God, and one river, and one tree of Life: three figures wherein are comprised the mysteries of the Incarnation, Baptism and Passion, whose leaves, that is to say, the words of the Gospel, bring healing to the nations through the teaching of a message that cannot fall to the ground.

18. *And all things whatsoever he does shall prosper.* Never again shall His gift and His statutes be set at naught, as they were in the case of Adam, who by his sin in breaking the Law lost the happiness of an assured immortality; but now, thanks to the redemption wrought by the tree of Life, that is, by the Passion of the Lord, all that happens to us is eternal and eternally conscious of happiness in virtue of our future likeness to that tree of Life. For all their doings shall prosper, being wrought no longer amid shift and change nor in human weakness, for corruption will be swallowed up in incorruption, weakness in endless life, the form of earthly flesh in the form of God. This tree, then, planted and yielding its fruit in its own season, shall that happy man resemble, himself being planted in the Garden, that what God has planted may abide, never to be

rooted up, in the Garden where all things done by God shall be guided to a prosperous issue, apart from the decay that belongs to human weakness and to time, and has to be uprooted.

19. The next point after the prophet had set forth the man's perfect happiness was for him to declare what punishment remained for the ungodly. Thus there ensues: *The ungodly are not so, but are like the dust which the wind drives away from the face of the earth.* The ungodly have no possible hope of having the image of the happy tree applied to them; the only lot that awaits them is one of wandering and winnowing, crushing, dispersion and unrest; shaken out of the solid framework of their bodily condition, they must be swept away to punishment in dust, a plaything of the wind. They shall not be dissolved into nothing, for punishment must find in them some stuff to work on, but ground into particles, imponderable, unsubstantial, dry, they shall be tossed to and fro, and make sport for the punishment that gives them never rest. Their punishment is recorded by the same Prophet in another place where he says: *I will beat them small as the dust before the wind, like the mire of the streets I will destroy them.*

Thus as there is an appointed type for happiness, so is there one for punishment. For as it is no hard task for the wind to scatter the dust, and as men who walk through the mud of the streets are hardly aware that they have been treading on it, so it is easy for the punishment of hell to destroy and disperse the ungodly, the logical result of whose sins is to melt them into mud and crush them into dust, reft of all solid substance, for dust and mud they are, and being merely mud and dust are good for nothing else than punishment.

20. And the Prophet, seeing that the change of their solid substance into dust will deprive them of all share in the boon of fruit to be bestowed upon the happy man in season by the tree, has accordingly added: *Therefore the ungodly shall not rise again in the Judgment.* The fact that they shall not rise again does not convey sentence of annihilation upon these men, for indeed they will exist as dust; it is the resurrection to Judgment that is denied them. Non-existence will not enable them to miss the pain of punishment; for while that which will be non-existent would escape punishment, they, on the other hand, will exist to be punished, for they will be dust. Now to become dust, whether by being dried to dust or ground to dust, involves not loss of the state of existence, but a change of state. But the fact that they will not rise again to Judgment makes it clear that they have lost, not the power to rise, but the privilege of rising to Judgment. Now what we are to understand by the privilege of rising again and being judged is declared by the Lord in the Gospels where He says: *He that believes in Me is not judged: he that believes not has been judged already. And this is the judgment, that the*

light has come into the world, and men loved the darkness rather than the light John 3:18-19 .

21. The terms of this utterance of the Lord are disturbing to inattentive hearers and careless, hasty readers. For by saying: *He that believes in Me shall not be judged*, He exempts believers, and by adding: *But he that believes not has been judged already*, He excludes unbelievers, from judgment. If, then, He has thus exempted believers and debarred unbelievers, allowing the chance of judgment neither to one class nor the other, how can He be considered consistent when he adds thirdly: *And this is the judgment, that the light has come into the world, and men loved the darkness rather than the light?* For there can apparently be no place left for judgment, since neither believers nor unbelievers are to be judged. Such no doubt will be the conclusion drawn by inattentive hearers and hasty readers. The utterance, however, has an appropriate meaning and a rational interpretation of its own.

22. He that believes, says Christ, is not judged. And is there any need to judge a believer? Judgment arises out of ambiguity, and where ambiguity ceases, there is no call for trial and judgment. Hence not even unbelievers need be judged, because there is no doubt about their being unbelievers; but after exempting believers and unbelievers alike from judgment, the Lord added a case for judgment and human agents upon whom it must be exercised. For

some there are who stand midway between the godly and the ungodly, having affinities to both, but strictly belonging to neither class, because they have come to be what they are by a combination of the two. They may not be assigned to the ranks of belief, because there is in them a certain infusion of unbelief; they may not be ranged with unbelief, because they are not without a certain portion of belief. For many are kept within the pale of the church by the fear of God; yet they are tempted all the while to worldly faults by the allurements of the world. They pray, because they are afraid; they sin, because it is their will. The fair hope of future life makes them call themselves Christians; the allurements of present pleasure make them act like heathen. They do not abide in ungodliness, because they hold the name of God in honour; they are not godly because they follow after things contrary to godliness. And they cannot help loving those things best which can never enable them to be what they call themselves, because their desire to do such works is stronger than their desire to be true to their name. And this is why the Lord, after saying that believers would not be judged and that unbelievers had been judged already, added that *This is the judgment, that the light has come into the world, and men loved the darkness rather than the light.*

These, then, are they whom the judgment awaits which unbelievers have already had passed upon them and believers do not need: because they have loved darkness more than light; not that they did not love the light too, but because their love of darkness is the more active. For when two loves are matched in rivalry, one always wins the preference; and their judgment arises from the fact that, though they loved Christ, they yet loved darkness more. These then will be judged; they are neither exempted from judgment like the godly, nor have they already been judged like the ungodly; but judgment awaits them for the love which they have deliberately preferred.

23. It is precisely the scheme and system thus laid down in the Gospel that the Prophet has followed, when he says: *Therefore the ungodly shall not rise again in the Judgement, nor sinners in the counsel of the righteous.* He leaves no judgment for the ungodly, because they have been judged already; on the other hand, he has refused to sinners, who as we showed in our former discourse are to be distinguished from the ungodly, the counsel of the righteous, because they are to be judged. For ungodliness causes the former to be judged beforehand, but sin keeps the latter to be judged hereafter. Thus ungodliness having already been judged is not admitted to the judgment of sinners, while again sinners, who, are yet to be judged, are deemed unworthy of enjoying the counsel of the righteous, who will not be judged.

24. The source of this distinction lies in the following words: *For the Lord knows the way of the righteous, but the way of the ungodly shall perish.*

Sinners do not come near the counsel of the righteous for this reason, that the Lord knows the way of the righteous. Now He knows, not by an advance from ignorance to knowledge, but because He condescends to know. For there is no play of human emotions in God that He should know or not know anything. The blessed Apostle Paul declared how we were known of God when he said: *If any man among you is a prophet or spiritual, let him take knowledge of the things which I write unto you, that they are of the Lord: but if any man does not know, he is not known* 1 Corinthians 14:37 .

Thus he shows that those are known of God who know the things of God: they are to come to be known when they know, that is, when they attain to the honour of being known through the merit of their known godliness, in order that the knowledge may be seen to be a growth on the part of him who is known, and not a growth on the part of one who knows not.

Now God shows clearly in the cases of Adam and Abraham that He does not know sinners, but does know believers. For it was said to Adam when he had sinned: *Adam, where are you* Genesis 3:9 ? Not because God knew not that the man whom He still had in the garden was there still, but to show, by his being asked where he was, that he was unworthy of God's knowledge by the fact of having sinned. But Abraham, after being for a long time unknown— the

23

word of God came to him when he was seventy years of age— was, upon his proving himself faithful to the Lord, admitted to intimacy with God by the following act of high condescension: *Now I know that you fear the Lord your God, and for My sake you have not spared your dearly loved son.*

God certainly was not ignorant of the faith of Abraham, which He had already reckoned to him for righteousness when he believed about the birth of Isaac: but now because he had given a signal instance of his fear in offering his son, he is at last known, approved, rendered worthy of being not unknown. It is in this way then that God both knows and knows not— Adam the sinner is not known, and Abraham the faithful is known, is worthy, that is, of being known by God Who surely knows all things. The way of the righteous, therefore, who are not to be judged is known by God: and this is why sinners, who are to be judged, are set far from their counsel; while the ungodly shall not rise again to judgment, because their way has perished, and they have already been judged by Him Who said: *The Father judges no man*, but has given all judgment unto the Son, our Lord Jesus Christ, Who is blessed for ever and ever. Amen.

For the end among the hymns, of the meaning of David when the Ziphims came and said to Saul: behold, is not David hid with us?

Save me, O God, by Your name, and judge me by Your power. Hear my prayer, O God; give ear unto the words of my mouth, and so on.

1. The doctrines of the Gospel were well known to holy and blessed David in his capacity of Prophet, and although it was under the Law that he lived his bodily life, he yet filled, as far as in him lay, the requirements of the Apostolic behest and justified the witness borne to him by God in the words: *I have found a man after My own heart, David, the son of Jesse.* He did not avenge himself upon his foes by war, he did not oppose force of arms to those that laid wait for him, but after the pattern of the Lord, Whose name and Whose meekness alike he foreshadowed, when he was betrayed he entreated, when he was in danger he sang psalms, when he incurred hatred he rejoiced; and for this cause he was found a man after God's own heart. For although twelve legions of angels might have come to the help of the Lord in His hour of passion, yet that He might perfectly fulfil His service of humble obedience, He surrendered Himself to suffering and weakness, only praying with the words: *Father into Your hands I commend My spirit.* Luke 23:46 After the same pattern, David, whose actual sufferings prophetically foretold the future sufferings of the Lord, opposed not his enemies either by word or act; in obedience to the command of the Gospel, he would not render evil for evil, in imitation of his Master's meekness, in his affliction, in his betrayal,

in his fight, he called upon the Lord and was content to use His weapons only in his contest with the ungodly.

2. Now to this Psalm is prefixed a title arising out of an historical event; but before the event is described we are instructed as to the scope, time and application of the incidents underlying it. First we have: *For the end of the meaning of that David.* Then there follows: *When the Ziphims came and said to Saul: behold, is not David hid with us?* Thus David's betrayal by the Ziphims awaits for its interpretation the end. This shows that what was actually being done to David contained a type of something yet to come; an innocent man is harassed by railing, a prophet is mocked by reviling words, one approved by God is demanded for execution, a king is betrayed to his foe. So the Lord was betrayed to Herod and Pilate by those very men in whose hands He ought to have been safe. The Psalm then awaits the end for its interpretation, and finds its meaning in the true David, in Whom is the end of the Law, that David who holds the keys and opens with them the gate of knowledge, in fulfilling the things foretold of Him by David.

3. The meaning of the proper name, according to the exact sense of the Hebrew, affords us no small assistance in interpreting the passage. *Ziphims* mean what we call sprinklings of the face; these were called in Hebrew *Ziphims*. Now, by the Law, sprinkling

was a cleansing from sins; it purified the people through faith by the sprinkling of blood, of which this same blessed David thus speaks: *You shall sprinkle me with hyssop and I shall be cleansed* ; the Law, through faith, providing as a temporary substitute, in the blood of whole burnt-offerings, a type of the sprinkling with the blood of the Lord, which was to be. But this people, like the people of the Ziphims, being sprinkled on their face and not in their faith, and receiving the cleansing drops on their lips and not in their hearts, turned faithless and traitors towards their David, as God had foretold by the Prophet: *This people honours Me with their lips, but their heart is far from Me.* They were ready to betray David because, the faith of their heart being dead, they had performed all the mystical ceremonies of the Law with deceitful face.

4. *Save me, O God, by Your Name, and judge me by Your power. Hear my prayer, O God; give ear unto the words of my mouth.*

The suffering of the Prophet David is, according to the account we have given of the title, a type of the Passion of our God and Lord Jesus Christ. This is why his prayer also corresponds in sense with the prayer of Him Who being the Word was made flesh: in such wise that He Who suffered all things after the manner of man, in everything He said, spoke after the manner of man; and He who bore the infirmities and took on Him the sins of men approached God in prayer with the humility proper to men. This interpretation, even though we be unwilling and slow to receive it, is required by the meaning and force of the words, so that there can be no doubt that everything in the Psalm is uttered by David as His mouthpiece. For he says: *Save me O God, by Your name.* Thus prays in bodily humiliation, using the words of His own Prophet, the Only-begotten Son of God, Who at the same time was claiming again the glory which He had possessed before the ages. He asks to be saved by the Name of God whereby He was called and wherein He was begotten, in order that the Name of God which rightly belonged to His former nature and kind might avail to save Him in that body wherein He had been born.

5. And because the whole of this passage is the utterance of One in the form of a servant— of a servant obedient unto the death of the Cross— which He took upon Him and for which He supplicates the saving help of the Name that belongs to God, and being sure of salvation by that Name, He immediately adds: *and judge Me by Your power.* For now as the reward for His humility in emptying Himself and assuming the form of a servant, in the same humility in which He had assumed it, He was asking to resume the form which He shared with God, having saved to bear the Name of God that humanity in which as God He had obediently condescended to be born. And in order to teach us

that the dignity of this Name whereby He prayed to be saved is something more than an empty title, He prays to be judged by the power of God. For a right award is the essential result of judgment, as the Scripture says: *Becoming obedient unto death , yea, the death of the Cross. Wherefore also God highly exalted Him and gave unto Him the name which is above every name.* Thus, first of all the name which is above every name is given unto Him; then next, this is a judgment of decisive force, because by the power of God, He, Who after being God had died as man, rose again from death as man to be God, as the Apostle says: *He was crucified from weakness, yet He lives by the power of God 2* Corinthians 13:4 *, and again: For I am not ashamed of the Gospel: for it is the power of God unto salvation to every one that believes.* Romans 1:16 For by the power of the Judgment human weakness is rescued to bear God's name and nature; and thus as the reward for His obedience He is exalted by the power of this judgment unto the saving protection of God's name; whence He possesses both the Name and the Power of God. Again, if the Prophet had begun this utterance in the way men generally speak, he would have asked to be judged by mercy or kindness, not by power. But judgment by power was a necessity in the case of One Who being the Son of God was born of a virgin to be Son of Man, and Who now being Son of Man was to have the Name and power of the Son of God restored to Him by the power of judgment.

6. Next there follows: *Hear my prayer, O God, give ear unto the words of my mouth*. The obvious thing for the Prophet to say was, *O God, hear me*. But because he is speaking as the mouthpiece of Him, Who alone knew how to pray, we are given a constantly reiterated demand that prayer shall be heard. The words of St. Paul teach us that no man knows how he ought to pray: *For we know not how to pray as we ought*. Man in his weakness, therefore, has no right to demand that his prayer shall be heard: for even the teacher of the Gentiles does not know the true object and scope of prayer, and that, after the Lord had given a model. What we are shown here is the perfect confidence of Him, Who alone sees the Father, Who alone knows the Father, Who alone can pray the whole night through— the Gospel tells us that the Lord continued all night in prayer— Who in the mirror of words has shown us the true image of the deepest of all mysteries in the simple words we use in prayer. And so, in making the demand that His prayer should be heard, he added, in order to teach us that this was the prerogative of His perfect confidence: *Give ear unto the words of My mouth*. Now can any man suppose that it is a human confidence which can thus desire that the words of his mouth should be heard? Those words, for instance, in which we express the motions and instincts of the mind, either when anger inflames us, or hatred moves us to slander, or pain to complaint, when flattery makes us fawn, when hope of gain or shame of the truth begets the lie, or resentment over

injury, the insult? Was there ever any man at all points so pure and patient in his life as not to be liable to these failings of human instability? He alone could confidently desire this Who did no sin, in Whose mouth was no deceit, Who gave His back to the smiters, Who turned not His cheek from the blow, Who did not resent scorn and spitting, Who never crossed the will of Him, to Whose Will ordering it all He gave in all points glad obedience.

7. He has next added the reason why He prays for His words to be heard: *For strangers are risen up against Me and violent men have sought after My soul; they have not set God before their eyes.* The Only-begotten Son of God, the Word of God and God the Word— although assuredly He could Himself do all things that the Father could, as He says: *What things soever the Father does, the Son also does in like manner* John 5:19, while the name describing the divine nature which was His inseparably involved the inseparable possession of divine power—yet in order that He might present to us a perfect example of human humility, both prayed for and underwent all things that are the lot of man. Sharing in our common weakness He prayed the Father to save Him, so that He might teach us that He was born man under all the conditions of man's infirmity. This is why He was hungry and thirsty, slept and was weary, shunned the assemblies of the ungodly, was sad and wept, suffered and died. And it was in order to make it clear that He was subject to all these

conditions, not by His nature, but by assumption, that when He had undergone them all He rose again. Thus all His complaints in the Psalms spring from a mental state belonging to our nature. Nor must it cause surprise if we take the words of the Psalms in this sense, seeing that the Lord Himself testified, if we believe the Gospel, that the Psalms spiritually foretold His Passion.

8. Now they were *strangers that rose up against Him.* For these are no sons of Abraham, nor sons of God, but a brood of vipers, servants of sin, a Canaanitish seed, their father an Amorite and their mother a daughter of Heth, inheriting diabolical desires from the devil their parent. Further it is the violent that seek after His soul; such as was Herod when he asked the chief priests where Christ should be born, such as was the whole synagogue when it bore false witness against Him. But in deeming this soul to be of human nature and weakness *they set not God before their eyes;* for God had stooped from that estate wherein He abode as God, even to the beginnings of human birth; that is, He became Son of Man Who before was the Son of God. For the Son of God is none other than He Who is Son of Man, and Son of Man not in partial measure but born so, the Form of God divesting Itself of that which It was and becoming that which It was not, that so It might be born into a soul and body of Its own. Hence He is both Son of God and Son of Man, hence both God and Man: in other words the Son of God was born

with the attributes derived from human birth, the Nature of God condescending to assume the nature of one born as man who is wholly moulded of soul and flesh. Wherefore strangers, when they rise up against Him, and the mighty, when they seek after that soul of His, which in the Gospels is often sad and cast down, set not God before their eyes, because God it was, and the Son of God existing from out the ages, that was born with the attributes of human nature, was born as man, that is, with our body and our soul, by a virgin birth; the mighty and glorious works He wrought never opened their eyes to the fact that the Son of Man Whose soul they were seeking had come to be man with a beginning of life after an eternal existence as Son of God.

9. The introduction of a pause marks a change of person. He no longer speaks but is addressed. For now the prophetic utterance assumes a general character. Thus immediately after the prayer addressed to God, he has added, in order that the confidence of the speaker might be understood to have obtained what He was asking even in the very moment of asking: *Behold, God is My helper and the Lord is the upholder of My soul. He has requited evil unto Mine enemies.* To each separate petition he has assigned its proper result, thus teaching us both that God does not neglect to hear, and that to look for a pledge of His pitifulness in hearing our several petitions is not a thing unreasonable. For to the words, *For strangers are risen up against Me,* the

corresponding statement is: *God is My helper;* while with regard to *and the violent have sought after My soul,* the exact result of the hearing of His prayer is expressed in the words: *and the Lord is the upholder of My soul;* lastly the statement, *they have not set God before their eyes,* is appropriately balanced by, *He has requited evil unto Mine enemies.* Thus God both gives help against those that rise up, and upholds the soul of His Holy One when it is sought by the violent, and when He is not set before the eyes, nor considered by the ungodly, He requites upon His enemies the very evils which they had wrought; so that while without thinking upon God they seek the soul of the righteous and rise up against Him, He is saved and upheld, and they find that He Whom, absorbed in their wicked works, they did not consider, avenges their malice by turning it against themselves.

10. Let pure religion, therefore, have this confidence, and doubt not that amid the persecutions at the hand of man and the dangers to the soul, it still has God for its helper, knowing that, if at length it comes to a violent and unjust death, the soul on leaving the tabernacle of the body finds rest with God its upholder; let it have, moreover, perfect assurance of requital in the thought that all evil deeds return upon the heads of those that work them. God cannot be charged with injustice, and perfect goodness is unstained by the impulses and motions of an evil will. He does not awaken mischief

out of malice, but requites it in vengeance; He does not inflict it because He wishes us ill, but He aims it against our sins. For these evils are universally appointed as instruments of retribution without destruction of life, such being the sternly just ordinance of that righteous judgment. But these evils are warded off from the righteous by the law of righteousness, and are turned back upon the unrighteous by the righteousness of that judgment. Each proceeding is equally just; for the righteous, because they are righteous, the warning exhibition of evil without actual infliction; for the wicked, because they so deserve, the punitive infliction of evil; the righteous will not suffer it, though it is displayed to them; the wicked will never cease to suffer it, because it is displayed to them.

11. After this there is a return to the Person of God, to Whom the petition was at the first addressed: *Destroy them by Your truth*. Truth confounds falsehood, and lying is destroyed by truth. We have shown that the whole of the foregoing prayer is the utterance of that human nature in which the Son of God was born; so here it is the voice of human nature calling upon God the Father to destroy His enemies in His truth. What this truth is, stands beyond doubt; it is of course He Who said: *I am the Life, the Way, the Truth*. John 14:6 And the enemies were destroyed by the truth when, for all their attempts to win Christ's condemnation by false witness, they heard that He was risen from the dead

and had to admit that He had resumed His glory in all the reality of Godhead. Ere long they found, in ruin and destruction by famine and war, their reward for crucifying God; for they condemned the Lord of Life to death, and paid no heed to God's truth displayed in Him through His glorious works. And thus the Truth of God destroyed them when He rose again to resume the majesty of His Father's Glory, and gave proof of the truth of that perfect Divinity which He possessed.

12. Now in view of our repeated, nay our unbroken assertion both that it was the Only-begotten Son of God Who was uplifted on the cross, and that He was condemned to death Who is eternal by virtue of the origin which is His by the nature which He derives from the eternal Father, it must be clearly understood that He was subjected to suffering of no natural necessity, but to accomplish the mystery of man's salvation; that He submitted to suffering of His own Will, and not under compulsion. And although this suffering did not belong to His nature as eternal Son, the immutability of God being proof against the assault of any derogatory disturbance, yet it was freely undertaken, and was intended to fulfil a penal function without, however, inflicting the pain of penalty upon the sufferer: not that the suffering in question was not of a kind to cause pain, but because the divine Nature feels no pain. God suffered, then, by voluntarily submitting to suffering; but although He underwent the sufferings in all the fullness of

their force, which necessarily causes pain to the sufferers, yet He never so abandoned the powers of His Nature as to feel pain.

13. For next there follows: *I will sacrifice unto You freely*. The sacrifices of the Law, which consisted of whole burnt-offerings and oblations of goats and of bulls, did not involve an expression of free will, because the sentence of a curse was pronounced on all who broke the Law. Whoever failed to sacrifice laid himself open to the curse. And it was always necessary to go through the whole sacrificial action because the addition of a curse to the commandment forbad any trifling with the obligation of offering. It was from this curse that our Lord Jesus Christ redeemed us, when, as the Apostle says: *Christ redeemed us from the curse of the law, being made curse for us, for it is written: cursed is every one that hangs on a tree*. Galatians 3:13 Thus He offered Himself to the death of the accursed that He might break the curse of the Law, offering Himself voluntarily a victim to God the Father, in order that by means of a voluntary victim the curse which attended the discontinuance of the regular victim might be removed. Now of this sacrifice mention is made in another passage of the Psalms: *Sacrifice and offering you would not, but a body have you prepared for Me* ; that is, by offering to God the Father, Who refused the legal sacrifices, the acceptable offering of the body which He received. Of which offering the holy Apostle thus speaks: *For this He did once for all when*

He offered Himself up Hebrews 7:27, securing complete salvation for the human race by the offering of this holy, perfect victim.

14. Then He gives thanks to God the Father for the accomplishment of all these acts: *I will give thanks unto Your name, O Lord, for it is good, for You have delivered Me out of all affliction.* He has assigned to each clause its strict fulfilment. Thus at the beginning He had said: *Save Me, O God, by Your name;* after the prayers had been heard it was right that there should follow a corresponding ascription of thanks, in order that confession might be made to His name by Whose name He had prayed to be saved, and that inasmuch as He had asked for help against the strangers that rose up against Him, He might set on record that He had received it in the burst of joy expressed in the words: *You have delivered Me out of all affliction.* Then in respect of the fact that the violent in seeking after His soul did not set God before their eyes, He has declared His eternal possession of unchangeable divinity in the words: *And My eye has looked down upon Mine enemies.* For the Only-begotten Son of God was not cut off by death. It is true that in order to take the whole of our nature upon Him He submitted to death, that is to the apparent severance of soul and body, and made His way even to the realms below, the debt which man must manifestly pay: but He rose again and abides for ever and looks down with an eye that death cannot dim upon His enemies,

being exalted unto the glory of God and born once more Son of God after becoming Son of Man, as He had been Son of God when He first became Son of Man, by the glory of His resurrection. He looks down upon His enemies to whom He once said: *Destroy this temple, and in three days I will build it up.* John 2:19 And so, now that this temple of His body has been built again, He surveys from His throne on high those who sought after His soul, and, set far beyond the power of human death, He looks down from heaven upon those who wrought His death, He who suffered death, yet could not die, the God-Man, our Lord Jesus Christ, Who is blessed for ever and ever. Amen.

O Lord, my heart is not exalted, neither have my eyes been lifted up.

1. This Psalm, a short one, which demands an analytical rather than a homiletical treatment, teaches us the lesson of humility and meekness. Now, as we have in a great number of other places spoken about humility, there is no need to repeat the same things here. Of course we are bound to bear in mind in how great need our faith stands of humility when we hear the Prophet thus speaking of it as equivalent to the performance of the highest works: *O Lord, my heart is not exalted.* For a troubled heart is the noblest sacrifice in the eyes of God. The heart, therefore, must not be lifted up by prosperity, but

humbly kept within the bounds of meekness through the fear of God.

2. *Neither have My eyes been lifted up.* The strict sense of the Greek here conveys a different meaning; οὐδὲ ἐμετεωρίσθησαν οἱ ὀφθαλμοί μου, that is, have not been lifted up from one object to look on another. Yet the eyes must be lifted up in obedience to the Prophet's words: *Lift up your eyes and see who has displayed all these things.* Isaiah 40:26 And the Lord says in the gospel: *Lift up your eyes, and look on the fields, that they are white unto harvest.* John 4:35 The eyes, then, are to be lifted up: not, however, to transfer their gaze elsewhere, but to remain fixed once for all upon that to which they have been raised.

3. Then follows: *Neither have I walked amid great things, nor amid wonderful things that are above me.* It is most dangerous to walk amid mean things, and not to linger amid wonderful things. God's utterances are great; He Himself is wonderful in the highest: how then can the psalmist pride himself as on a good work for not walking amid great and wonderful things? It is the addition of the words, *which are above me,* that shows that the walking is not amid those things which men commonly regard as great and wonderful. For David, prophet and king as he was, once was humble and despised and unworthy to sit at his father's table; but he found favour with God, he was anointed to be king, he was

inspired to prophesy. His kingdom did not make him haughty, he was not moved by hatreds: he loved those that persecuted him, he paid honour to his dead enemies, he spared his incestuous and murderous children. In his capacity of sovereign he was despised, in that of father he was wounded, in that of prophet he was afflicted; yet he did not call for vengeance as a prophet might, nor exact punishment as a father, nor requite insults as a sovereign. And so he did not walk amid things great and wonderful which were above him.

4. Let us see what comes next: *If I was not humble-minded but have lifted up my soul.* What inconsistency on the Prophet's part! He does not lift up his heart: he does lift up his soul. He does not walk amid things great and wonderful that are above him; yet his thoughts are not mean. He is exalted in mind and cast down in heart. He is humble in his own affairs: but he is not humble in his thought. For his thought reaches to heaven, his soul is lifted up on high. But his heart, *out of which proceed,* according to the Gospel, *evil thoughts, murders, adulteries, fornications, thefts, false witness, railings* Matthew 15:19, is humble, pressed down beneath the gentle yoke of meekness. We must strike a middle course, then, between humility and exaltation, so that we may be humble in heart but lifted up in soul and thought.

5. Then he goes on: *Like a weaned child upon his mother's breast, so will you reward my soul.* We are told that when Isaac was weaned Abraham made a feast because now that he was weaned he was on the verge of boyhood and was passing beyond milk food. The Apostle feeds all that are imperfect in the faith and still babes in the things of God with the milk of knowledge. Thus to cease to need milk marks the greatest possible advance. Abraham proclaimed by a joyful feast that his son had come to stronger meat, and the Apostle refuses bread to the carnal-minded and those that are babes in Christ. And so the Prophet prays that God, because he has not lifted up his heart, nor walked amid things great and wonderful that are above him, because he has not been humble-minded but did lift up his soul, may reward his soul, lying like a weaned child upon his mother: that is to say that he may be deemed worthy of the reward of the perfect, heavenly and living bread, on the ground that by reason of his works already recorded he has now passed beyond the stage of milk.

6. But he does not demand this living bread from heaven for himself alone, he encourages all mankind to hope for it by saying: *Let Israel hope in the Lord from henceforth and for evermore.* He sets no temporal limit to our hope, he bids our faithful expectation stretch out into infinity. We are to hope for ever and ever, winning the hope of future life through the hope of our present life which we have in Christ

Jesus our Lord, Who is blessed for ever and ever.
Amen.

Made in the USA
Coppell, TX
13 January 2020